The Word Wizard's Book of ADJECTIVES

Robin Johnson

Crabtree
Publishing
Company
www.crabtreebooks.com

Word Wizard

Author
Robin Johnson

Publishing plan research and development
Reagan Miller, Crabtree Publishing Company

Editorial director
Kathy Middleton

Project coordinator
Kelly Spence

Editor
Anastasia Suen

Proofreader and indexer
Wendy Scavuzzo

Photo research
Robin Johnson, Katherine Berti

Design & prepress
Katherine Berti

Print coordinator
Katherine Berti

Photographs
All images from Shutterstock

Library and Archives Canada Cataloguing in Publication

Johnson, Robin (Robin R.), author
    The word wizard's book of adjectives / Robin Johnson.

(Word wizard)
Includes index.
Issued in print and electronic formats.
ISBN 978-0-7787-1304-3 (bound).--ISBN 978-0-7787-1312-8 (pbk.).--
ISBN 978-1-4271-7762-9 (pdf).--ISBN 978-1-4271-7758-2 (html)

    1. English language--Adjective--Juvenile literature. I. Title.

PE1241.J64 2014   j428.2   C2014-903813-5
                                         C2014-903814-3

Library of Congress Cataloging-in-Publication Data

Johnson, Robin (Robin R.) author.
  The Word Wizard's book of adjectives / Robin Johnson.
    p. cm. -- (Word Wizard)
  Includes index.

 ISBN 978-0-7787-1304-3 (reinforced library binding) --
ISBN 978-0-7787-1312-8 (pbk.) -- ISBN 978-1-4271-7762-9 (electronic pdf) --
ISBN 978-1-4271-7758-2 (electronic html)
1. English language--Adjective--Juvenile literature. 2. English language--
Parts of speech--Juvenile literature. 3. English language--Grammar--
Juvenile literature. I. Title. II. Title: Book of adjectives.

 PE1241.J64 2014
 425'.5--dc23
                              2014027802

Crabtree Publishing Company

www.crabtreebooks.com   1-800-387-7650

Printed in the U.S.A./092014/JA20140811

Published in Canada
Crabtree Publishing
616 Welland Ave.
St. Catharines, Ontario
L2M 5V6

Published in the United States
Crabtree Publishing
PMB 59051
350 Fifth Avenue, 59th Floor
New York, New York 10118

Published in the United Kingdom
Crabtree Publishing
Maritime House
Basin Road North, Hove
BN41 1WR

Published in Australia
Crabtree Publishing
3 Charles Street
Coburg North
VIC 3058

Contents

Magical words

Words are magical things! They make you happy when you are sad. They turn bad days into good days. They even change ugly frogs into handsome princes! The Word Wizards can make magic. They need your help to learn some new magic words, though.

one   slimy   handsome
loving   happy   green

magical

pretty

ugly

pink

Some words are short. Others are long. They are all magical!

What are words for?

There are all kinds of words. We use words called **adjectives** to describe things. We use words to share our bright ideas. We tell funny jokes. We sing silly songs. We listen to bedtime stories. What else can we do with words?

Nests built by

Most birds build nests in which they lay their eggs. When the baby birds hatch, or break out of their eggs, they are safe from predators. Most bird parents feed their chicks, or baby birds, until they learn to fly and find their own food.

Some birds build nests in high places, such as trees, chimneys, or the tops of poles. This stork nest is built of sticks at the top of a little trunk.

10

What are adjectives?

Adjectives are words that tell us more about things. They describe words called **nouns**. Nouns name people, animals, places, things, or ideas. The word "apple" is a noun. The words "red" and "crisp" are adjectives. We could use those adjectives to describe an apple.

Food for thought

We use our five senses to describe nouns. Adjectives tell us how nouns look, sound, smell, taste, or feel. Think of the last food you ate. What color was it? Was it sweet or salty? Was it soft or crunchy? Think of adjectives to describe your favorite foods.

Word Wizard in training

Which sentence below has adjectives? Help the Word Wizard find them! Remember to look for words that use the five senses.

The furry little monkey is eating a tasty yellow banana.

The boy is swinging like a monkey!

All kinds of adjectives

There are all sorts of adjectives! Some tell what kinds of things nouns are. You could say you went to a birthday party. There were blue balloons there. The word "birthday" describes the party. The word "blue" tells about the balloons.

How many?

Other adjectives tell how many things there are. You could say there were many kids at the party. You ate three pieces of birthday cake. The word "many" describes the number of kids at the party. The word "three" tells that you ate too much cake!

Word Wizard in training

Help the Word Wizard describe the picture. How many children are at the party? What shape is the cake? What color are the balloons? What other adjectives can you use to describe the picture?

Joining words

We join adjectives and other words together. The words form **sentences**. Sentences are complete thoughts or ideas. They are made up of many types of words. Most sentences have adjectives. Some do not.

Before or after

Adjectives work with nouns in sentences. They usually come before the nouns. We can say, "The <u>cute</u> puppy chases the <u>bouncy</u> ball." Sometimes adjectives come after nouns. We can say, "The puppy is <u>cute</u> when it chases the <u>bouncy</u> ball." How do you find adjectives? You look for words that describe people, animals, places, things, or ideas.

Word Wizard in training

Help the Word Wizard find the adjectives in these sentences. Do they come before or after the nouns?

The hungry puppy is chewing an old slipper.

The kitten is tired. It is sleeping in a soft bed.

Comparing words

We use adjectives to **compare** nouns. Comparing means telling what is the same or different. We use some adjectives to compare two nouns. We add "er" to these adjectives. The words "taller" and "grumpier" are adjectives. They compare two people, places, or things.

Sometimes we cannot add "er" to adjectives. "Funner" is not a word. We would say "more fun" instead.

Which drawing looks happier? Which drawing looks sadder?

More than two

We use other adjectives to compare more than two nouns. We add "est" to these adjectives. The words "loudest" and "laziest" are adjectives.

We cannot add "est" to some adjectives. "Afraidest" is not a word. We would say "most afraid" instead.

Which ice-cream cone is tallest? Which one would you like to eat?

Antonyms

Some adjectives are **antonyms**. Antonyms are words with totally different meanings. They are also called **opposites**. The words "good" and "bad" are antonyms. The words "hot" and "cold" are antonyms. What are some other antonyms?

The children are selling cold lemonade on a hot day.

Telling stories

Antonyms help us tell stories. You could say you got a pair of sneakers. You really needed them. You could also say you got new sneakers. Your old sneakers were really stinky. The words "new" and "old" are antonyms. They tell that the shoes are very different.

Word Wizard
in training

Look at the chart below.
Use your finger to match
up the antonyms.

up	weak
clean	soft
hard	full
heavy	down
strong	dirty
empty	light

Synonyms

Some adjectives are **synonyms**. Synonyms mean the same thing or nearly the same thing as other words. The words "little" and "small" are synonyms. The words "big" and "large" are synonyms. They are words with the same meanings.

Not boring

Would you like a story that used the same adjectives? No! It would be boring! It would be dull! It would be dreary! Synonyms make stories more fun to read. They work like magic. They turn boring stories into interesting stories.

Word Wizard
in training

Show the Word Wizard
which caption has synonyms.
You are smart. You are clever.
You are bright. You can do it!

The clown is sad.
He is sad because
he lost his balloons.

The clown is silly.
He makes the children
laugh with his goofy tricks.

Not quite the same

Some adjectives have **similar** meanings. Similar means they are sort of the same. They are not exactly the same, though. How would you describe dinosaurs? Would you say they were large? Or would you say they were huge?

The girl is much bigger than her toy dinosaurs. She looks gigantic! Do the dinosaurs seem small or tiny?

Shades of meaning

The words "large" and "huge" both mean "big."

The word "huge" tells us dinosaurs were really big!

The words have different **shades of meaning**. That means they are similar but have small differences.

Understanding the differences helps us tell our stories.

Some dinosaurs are creepy or frightening.

This dinosaur is not scary at all!

Sorting words

We can sort words to understand shades of meaning. Some adjectives have weaker meanings. Other adjectives have stronger meanings. We can put them in order from weakest to strongest.

Weaker words	Stronger words	Strongest words
good →	great →	amazing
thin	skinny	scrawny
dusty	dirty	filthy
mean	cruel	evil
mad	angry	furious
pretty	beautiful	gorgeous
chilly	cold	freezing
bad	awful	terrible

Word Wizard
in training

Help the Word Wizard describe this picture. Do the boys look happy? Or do they look thrilled? Do you think they are hungry? Or are they starving? Think of weak and strong words to describe the picture.

Painting a picture

What things do you see in this picture? Use adjectives to describe them.

Adjectives help us **communicate** with others. To communicate is to share ideas and information. Adjectives help us describe how things look, sound, smell, taste, or feel. They help us tell stories. They let us paint pictures with our words.

Word Wizard
in training

You can be a Word Wizard too! Draw or paint a picture of yourself. Then write down adjectives that describe you. Are you short or tall? Are you funny or serious? Try to think of many different adjectives. They will help others learn all about you!

Learning more

Books

Adjectives (Grammar Basics) by Kate Riggs. Creative Paperbacks, 2013.

A Hat Full of Adjectives (Words I Know) by Bette Blaisdell. A+ Books, 2014.

Bowling Alley Adjectives (Grammar All-Stars) by Doris Fisher. Gareth Stevens Publishing, 2008.

If You Were an Adjective (Word Fun) by Michael Dahl. Nonfiction Picture Books, 2006.

Quirky, Jerky, Extra Perky: More about Adjectives (Words Are CATegorical) by Brian P. Cleary. First Avenue Editions, 2009.

Websites

Compare adjectives and have fun at this PBS Kids website.
http://pbskids.org/lions/games/trampolini.html

Visit this website for an adjective game and printable worksheets.
www.turtlediary.com/grade-1-games/ela-games/describing-words.html

Go on an adjective adventure at this website.
www.sheppardsoftware.com/grammar/adjectives.htm

Words to know

adjective (AJ-ik-tiv) A word that tells how a noun looks, sounds, smells, tastes, or feels

antonym (AN-tuh-nim) A word that means the opposite of another word

communicate (kuh-MYOO-ni-keyt) To share ideas and information

compare (kuhm-PAIR) To tell what is the same or different

noun (noun) A word that names a person, animal, place, thing, or idea

opposite (OP-uh-sit) Totally different

senses (SEN-sez) Actions of the body that help us learn about our surroundings

sentence (SEN-tns) A complete thought or idea

shades of meaning (sheyds uhv MEE-ning) Small differences in the meaning of words

similar (SIM-uh-ler) Almost the same as someone or something else

synonym (SIN-uh-nim) A word that means the same thing or nearly the same thing as another word

Index